Blackbeard

Copyright © 2016 by Quelle Histoire / quellehistoire.com
Published by Roaring Brook Press
Roaring Brook Press is a division of Holtzbrinck Publishing Holdings Limited Partnership
175 Fifth Avenue, New York, NY 10010
mackids.com

Library of Congress Control Number: 2017957511
ISBN 978-1-250-16605-0

Our books may be purchased in bulk for promotional, educational, or business use.
Please contact your local bookseller or the Macmillan Corporate and Premium Sales Department
at (800) 221-7945 ext. 5442 or by e-mail at MacmillanSpecialMarkets@macmillan.com.

First published in France in 2016 by Quelle Histoire, Paris
First U.S. edition, 2018

Text: Clémentine V. Baron
Translation: Catherine Nolan
Illustrations: Bruno Wennagel, Nuno Alves Rodrigues, Mathieu Ferret, Claire Martin, Paul Cotoni,
Clara Morineau, Iris Mangin

Printed in China by RR Donnelley Asia Printing Solutions Ltd., Dongguan City, Guangdong Province
10 9 8 7 6 5 4 3 2 1

Blackbeard

Roaring Brook Press
New York

The Golden Age of Pirates

Long ago, pirates roamed the seas. They chased down cargo ships loaded with gold, tobacco, and sugar. Then they attacked!

The most feared pirate of all was Edward Teach, better known as Blackbeard.

———

1650–1730

Serving Queen Anne

Edward was born in Bristol, England, around the year 1680. When he was about twenty years old, England went to war. Edward went, too! He became a privateer. Privateers were like pirates. But during a war, their rulers allowed them to attack and steal from enemy ships.

These privateers served the Queen of England. They captured ships and seized the cargo for Queen Anne.

———

1680–1713

Joining a Crew

The war ended in 1714. Queen Anne didn't need privateers anymore. Now what?

Edward had learned a lot at sea. He could sail. He could shoot a pistol. He could swing a cutlass—the short, curved sword sailors used.

Edward decided to become a pirate! He joined the crew of pirate captain Benjamin Hornigold.

———

1714–1717

Becoming Blackbeard

Benjamin helped Edward capture the French ship *La Concorde*. Edward turned it into his own pirate ship! He renamed it the *Queen Anne's Revenge.*

Edward gave himself a new name, too—Captain Blackbeard, because he had a thick, dark, scraggly beard.

1717

The Terror of the Seas

The *Queen Anne's Revenge* was a frightening ship. It had forty big guns. Its flag showed a skeleton stabbing a heart.

Sometimes, when ships were attacked by the *Queen Anne's Revenge*, they gave up without a fight!

Blackbeard was as scary as his ship. He wove cannon fuses into his beard. Then he lit them up. People said he looked like a demon, with flames all around his face!

———

1717–1718

The Charleston Blockade

Captain Blackbeard's fame grew. He captured more and more ships. He commanded three hundred men. In 1718, Blackbeard used his ships to block off the port in Charleston, South Carolina. For days, any other ships that wanted to go in or out had to give Blackbeard their cargo!

But as fierce as he was, Blackbeard would sometimes let his prisoners go free. He took care of his crew, too.

—

May 1718

The End of the
Queen Anne's Revenge

Blackbeard finally left Charleston. But he didn't get far. His ship ran into a sandbank!

Blackbeard abandoned the *Queen Anne's Revenge*. He sailed away on a smaller boat called a sloop.

Was it an accident? Some people think Blackbeard wrecked his ship on purpose. That way he could leave his crew behind and take all the loot for himself!

———

May 1718

No More Captain Blackbeard?

Blackbeard was done being a pirate—or so he said. He moved to Bath, North Carolina. He began calling himself Edward Teach again. He even married a woman in town.

But Blackbeard did not like life on dry land. A few weeks later, he returned to sea. Captain Blackbeard was back!

———

June 1718

The Chase

Shipowners were tired of having their ships attacked. They wanted Blackbeard stopped.

A British navy officer named Robert Maynard was sent to find Blackbeard. Robert set sail in a warship called the *Pearl*.

Robert caught up with Blackbeard on November 22, 1718. The two men met face-to-face!

———

November 1718

The Battle

Robert pulled out his pistol. He shot Blackbeard! The pirate fought back. He swung his cutlass and knocked Robert's pistol out of his hand. Blackbeard was about to win the fight.

Then a sailor from the *Pearl* stabbed Blackbeard with a knife! Blackbeard stood up and kept fighting. But he lost. After he was wounded many more times, he finally fell down dead.

Captain Blackbeard was gone. Or was he?

Legend has it that Blackbeard's ghost haunts the high seas to this day!

November 1718

1670

1680
Edward
Teach is born
in England.

1701
England goes
to war. Edward
becomes a
privateer.

1714
The war
is over.

1716
Edward joins
Benjamin
Hornigold's
crew.

1713
A treaty is
signed to end
the war.

1716
Edward decides
to become
a pirate.

1717
Edward becomes Captain Blackbeard.

1718
May: Blackbeard blocks port of Charleston.

1718
June: Blackbeard moves to Bath and gets married.

1718
November 22: Blackbeard dies.

1717
November 28: Edward and Benjamin capture *La Concorde*.

1717
Blackbeard's fame grows. He captures three more ships.

1718
May: Blackbeard abandons the *Queen Anne's Revenge*.

1718
June: Blackbeard goes back to sea.

1720

Blackbeard's Journey

1

5
6
4
3

2

1 Bristol

The town in England where Edward Teach was born.

2 Nassau

A city in the Bahamas where Edward met Benjamin Hornigold. Nassau was the "pirate capital" until 1718.

3 Charleston

In Blackbeard's day, this U.S. city was a port town in the colony of South Carolina.

4 Beaufort Bay

This is the spot where Blackbeard's ship, the *Queen Anne's Revenge*, ran aground.

5 Bath

Blackbeard settled here during his short break from pirate life.

6 Bay of Ocracoke

Robert Maynard caught up with Blackbeard in this bay off the coast of North Carolina.

People to Know

Queen Anne
(1665–1714)

The queen of Great Britain during the
War of the Spanish Succession. Privateers
fought in her name.

Benjamin Hornigold
(Unknown–1719)

This pirate sailed alongside Blackbeard
from the beginning of 1716 to the end
of 1717.

Charles Eden
(1673–1722)

The second governor of North Carolina, he agreed not to arrest Blackbeard when the pirate moved to Bath. (Blackbeard offered him a share of his loot!)

Robert Maynard
(1684–1751)

This British Royal Navy lieutenant caught Blackbeard in 1718.

....

There is no evidence that Blackbeard killed any of his captives. And he may have given the captain of *La Concorde* another ship after stealing his!

....

Benjamin Hornigold was a pirate until 1717. Then he switched sides and became a pirate hunter.

....

....

Blackbeard was famous for his beard and his three-cornered hat.

In 1996, the wreck from the *Queen Anne's Revenge* was found off the coast of North Carolina.

Available Now

Muhammad Ali

Neil Armstrong

Blackbeard

Coco Chanel

Charlie Chaplin

Cleopatra

Marie Curie

Albert Einstein

Abraham Lincoln

Nelson Mandela

Isaac Newton

Rosa Parks

Coming Soon

Anne Frank

Gandhi

Frida Kahlo

Martin Luther King, Jr.